MEL BAY PRESENTS

FAMOUS SOLOS & DUETS
for the
'UKULELE

edited & arranged
by
JOHN KING

CD contents

1	Loke Lani [2:24]	9	Spanish Fandango [1:42]	17	Ei Nei [2:26]
2	Haele [1:02]	10	The Blue Bells of Scotland [1:39]	18	Aloha O'e [1:30]
3	Hone A Ka Wai [1:37]	11	Leilani [2:23]	19	Serenade of the Ukuleles [1:33]
4	Polka Mazurka [1:04]	12	Banjo Schottische [1:18]	20	Timothy at the Husking Bee [2:12]
5	Ka Wehi [0:56]	13	Lauia [1:58]	21	Aloha Quickstep [1:41]
6	Funiculi-Funicolà [2:21]	14	Wailana [3:18]	22	Petite Valse [2:14]
7	Hene [1:51]	15	El Recuerdo [1:42]		
8	Ahi Wela [1:52]	16	Hawai'i Pono'i [2:23]		

Performer: John King
Recorded at Paul Oldack Productions, Tampa, Florida
Engineer: Sue Bober

1 2 3 4 5 6 7 8 9 0

Visit us on the Web at www.melbay.com — E-mail us at email@melbay.com

PRINCESS LYDIA LILIʻUOKALANI, *ca. 1880's.*
(Hawaiʻi State Archives)

CONTENTS

MADEIRAN GIRL WITH A *MACHETE, ca. 1900.*
(Collection of the Author)

PREFACE

THE 'UKULELE

The 'ukulele is not an indigenous Hawaiian instrument but was introduced into the Islands by the Portuguese at some date prior to the beginning of the 20th century. Most scholars fix the date of introduction at 1879, though it could have been earlier. It was in late August of that year that the three men most closely identified with the early history of the little four-stringed guitar arrived in Honolulu: Augusto Dias (1842-1915), Jose do Espirito Santo (1850-1905), and Manuel Nunes (1843-1922). Cabinet makers from Madeira, who eventually set up shop in Honolulu after paying off their passage and that of their families by fulfilling labor contracts with the Hawaiian sugar industry, Dias, Espirito Santo and Nunes were all advertising their services for making furniture and stringed instruments by 1886. Initially Dias and Nunes advertised *Machets*, or *machetes*, the name by which the predecessor to the 'ukulele was known in Madeira. Within seven years of the arrival of the Portuguese, the *machete* had become known in Honolulu as the taropatch fiddle, a term which then quickly became identified with a larger five string instrument, also from Madeira, and known there as the *rajao*; since about 1915 the name taropatch has been reserved for a larger, four-course, eight-string 'ukulele. The first evidence of the name 'ukulele' (though spelled *ukelele*) being applied to the smaller four-string instrument dates from an 1891 travel book by Helen Mather. She noted the playing of the "ukelele" and five string taropatch to accompany a *hula* performed on board a ship bound to Honolulu from San Francisco, a city which figured prominently in the popularization of Hawaiian music generally and the 'ukulele in particular.

Early mainland appearances of the 'ukulele were noted at the many world's fairs held between 1893 and 1915. A quartet of Hawaiian performers known as the Volcano Singers entertained visitors to the *Kilau'ea* Cyclorama during the 1893 World's Columbian Exposition in Chicago. They accompanied themselves with guitars, five-string taropatch and 'ukulele. The California Mid-Winter Fair of 1894, held in San Francisco, also featured a *Kilau'ea* exhibit and a Hawaiian Village with Hawaiians playing the "taropatch" as well as giving lessons to enchanted San Franciscans. In 1897, the New York *Times* reported on "Hawaii's Ex-Queen's Concert", a by-invitation-only performance held in her rooms at the Shoreham in Washington, D. C. The *Times* noted that deposed Queen Lili'uokalani would be singing "songs of her nation" and playing autoharp and would be joined by Grace Hilborn, the daughter of a member of the U.S. House of Representatives from San Francisco, who would be singing Hawaiian songs and accompanying herself on the 'ukulele "a native instrument that looks and sounds like a diminutive guitar." By 1898, the 'ukulele had become so associated with Hawaiians and their music that Lili'uokalani referred to it as "our instrument."

Espirito Santo was the first to advertise 'ukulele (and taropatch fiddles) in the Honolulu City Directory, in 1898, the same year Dias advertised "instruments made of Hawaiian woods." During the first decade of the new century these 'made in Hawai'i' adaptations of the Portuguese *machete* were introduced to mainlanders in numerous ways. Tourists returning home from a visit to the 'Paradise of the Pacific' brought 'ukulele back with them as souvenirs and gifts. Hawaiians entertained at the 1901 Pan-American Exposition in Buffalo and the 1909 Alaska-Yukon-Pacific Exposition in Seattle. Hawaiian performers, including the Honolulu Students, Ellis Hawaiians, and Joseph Kekuku (father of the steel guitar) were highly sought after on the Chautauqua and Lyceum circuits and performed throughout the mainland. And the fledgling record industry, lead by

Victor, Columbia, and Edison, began recording and selling Hawaiian music between 1905 and 1910. When Mr. & Mrs. Jack London sailed into Honolulu Harbor aboard the *Snark* with a Victor and 300 disks in May, 1907, and proceeded to play recordings of Hawaiian music for their guests "none of [whom] had heard Hawaiian music on the phonograph [they] clapped their hands over the hulas like joyous children."

Budding interest in the 'ukulele and Hawaiian music blossomed after the premiere of Walter Morosco's production of *The Bird of Paradise*, a play by Richard Walton Tully, which opened in Los Angeles in the early Fall of 1911. The play—which featured a quintet of Hawaiian musicians in the cast, singing and playing their instruments nearly non-stop—traveled to Chicago and Rochester before opening on Broadway in January, 1912. Backed by a group of San Francisco businessmen, including the sugar king Claus Spreckels, *The Bird of Paradise* toured the nation and was one of the most successful plays of the time; much of the credit for that success was attributed to the "weird and sensuous music." In 1914, Leonardo Nunes (1874-1944), son of 'ukulele pioneer Manuel Nunes, opened a shop and began making instruments under his own name in Los Angeles. In that same year, five 'ukulele methods were published in California: two in San Francisco (Bailey, Keech) and three in Los Angeles (DeLano, Kealakai, Kia). As if to underscore this burgeoning interest retail giant Sears, Roebuck & Co. offered "Hawaiian" 'ukulele for the first time in its Fall 1914 catalogue, stating "the ukulele is creating a sensation in this country, especially on the Pacific Coast, where it is exceedingly popular."

Largely regarded as the seminal event in popularizing the 'ukulele and Hawaiian music on the mainland, the Panama-Pacific International Exposition opened in San Francisco in 1915. Billed as a celebration of the opening of the Panama Canal, the Expo was also the symbolic rebirth of San Francisco following the devastation of the 1906 earthquake and fire. It was a huge event which as many as 17 million people attended. The scope and variety of the exhibits and amusements were astonishing. In *The Story of the Exposition* historian Frank Morton Todd called the Hawaiian Building "one of the most brilliant and beautiful elements of the Exposition," featuring performances of Hawaiian music from an interior gazebo festooned with Hawaiian flora. In addition to the Hawaiian Building and a special "Hawaiian Day" held on Kamehameha's birthday, the P. P. I. E. offered two other distinct performance venues for Hawaiian music: the Hawaiian Gardens in the Horticultural Building, and the Hawaiian Village on the "Zone" (midway). Todd commented, "people were about ready for a new sensation in popular music at the time of the Exposition, and the sweet voices of the Hawaiians raised in those haunting minor melodies ... were enough to start another musical vogue. To this the exhibit of Jonah Kumalae of Honolulu ministered, for he showed Hawaiian ukuleles and taro-patch fiddles."

Following the P. P. I. E. the number of 'ukulele manufacturers increased dramatically on the mainland, and in the Islands existing makers struggled to meet demand. All the major music houses in the U.S., including Oliver Ditson and all its branches on the East Coast, Lyon & Healy in Chicago, and Sherman, Clay & Co. in California, were engaged in making or distributing 'ukulele. High-end guitar makers C.F. Martin & Co. had entered the fray by 1917, marketing three styles of 'ukulele. Orders for instruments in the mail-order catalogues of Sears, Roebuck & Co. and Montgomery Ward surged. In 1918, four years following their initial offering of just two styles of 'ukulele, Sears offered no fewer than sixteen different "Hawaiian Instruments" including birch wood, mahogany, and *koa* wood 'ukulele, eight-string taro patch fiddles and banjo-ukes. In 1924 Cliff Edwards appeared in George and Ira Gershwin's first Broadway show, *Lady Be Good*, playing the 'ukulele and singing alongside Fred and Adele Astaire. At least one performer, Frank Lane, hoped to cheat oblivion by billing himself in 1925 as "one of the few remaining entertainers who work without the aid of a ukelele."

From obscurity to international fame, the phenomenal popularity of the 'ukulele and Hawaiian music proved the predictions of at least two critics wrong. In 1850 John A. Dix, a former U.S. Senator from New York (and later governor of the same state), published a book of his travels in Madeira. He commented on the ubiquity of the little four-string guitar, noting however, that "its music ... is thin and meagre. It is not probable that the *machete* will ever emigrate from Madeira. It is the most common instrument here; but I doubt very much whether it would be, if this were not its birthplace." John R. Musick, writing in 1898 in a book entitled *Hawaii ... Our New Possessions*, remarked "If the natives have a special talent for anything, it is music. Some of them have composed, but their music is as narrow as their own sphere, and will never become widely popular." Of the three original Portuguese 'ukulele makers, only Nunes lived to see the instrument become popular. Espirito Santo died of blood poisoning in 1905, and Dias succumbed to tuberculosis in February of 1915, just 15 days before the opening of the P. P. I. E. Nunes' death from heart failure in 1922 was reported on the front pages of both Honolulu newspapers, probably due to a successful marketing campaign begun about 1910, that attributed the 'invention' of the 'ukulele to the young cabinet maker in 1879.

THE METHODS

One Hawaiian who believed the 'ukulele was "not an invention but rather a creation" was Ernest Ka'ai (1881-1962),

the "most eminent of Hawaiian musicians" and arguably the most influential musical figure in *Hawai'i* in the first quarter of the 20th century. A gifted performer on many instruments including the mandolin, guitar and 'ukulele, Ka'ai was also an impresario, teacher, publisher and recording artist and he owned an 'ukulele manufacturing company. Known in Honolulu as the "Father of the Ukulele" Ka'ai was said to have been the first musician "to play a complete melody with chords" on that instrument. He also wrote the earliest known 'ukulele method. Although its location is now uncertain, Hawaiian music authority Amy Stillman catalogued the (presumed) first edition of Ka'ai's *The Ukulele, A Hawaiian Guitar and How to Play It* in the 1980's. It was published by Wall, Nichols Co. of Honolulu in 1906. An advertisement for the "Kaai Music School" from the 1909 Honolulu telephone directory stated that Ka'ai taught the 'ukulele "from Method." In addition to these references, 'ukulele historian Tom Walsh owns an original receipt dated 1906 from the Kaai Music Studios (and signed by Ka'ai) for several lessons and an "ukulele book": undoubtedly the 1906 "ghost" imprint.

In 1909, the Oliver Ditson Co. of Boston published a *Method for the Ukulele (Hawaiian Guitar)* edited by T.H. Rollinson. Thomas Rollinson (1844-1928) was a cornet player, band leader and composer of over 400 original works and 1,500 arrangements for band. In 1887 the Oliver Ditson Co. employed him as an arranger for the publication department, a position he held until his death in 1928. There is no evidence that Rollinson had any experience with *Hawai'i* and its language, or Hawaiian music and musical instruments. It is likely his method is based on the earlier work of Ernest Ka'ai; unfortunately,

7

beyond the descriptive subtitle "Hawaiian Guitar" mentioned in the Stillman citation, it is not possible to compare the Ditson method with Ka'ai's 1906 tutor. Why Ditson would not have simply reproduced the Ka'ai method is a matter for speculation, but there had been a working relationship between Ditson and Wall, Nichols Co. since at least 1901, when both published Charles Hopkins' *Aloha Collection of Hawaiian Songs*. Probably produced to support sales of *'ukulele* at Ditson's stores in Boston, New York and Philadelphia (a 1910 Ditson advertisement for "Odd Musical Instruments" in the New York *Times* included *'ukulele*), the Ditson method was 16 pages long and included 8 solo pieces in standard notation, none of which were Hawaiian. One piece was to be "played in the native style with sweep strokes [strums]" and despite stating that the *'ukulele* was used "principally for accompanying songs," Rollinson included none. The pedagogical material was confined to scales, "double-stops" and directions for playing three different "strokes". Perhaps the most remarkable thing about this primer was its early appearance in the mainland market, pre-dating other similar publications by 5 years.

Several observations can be made regarding the Ditson method and the relatively common Ka'ai *Revised Edition* published by Wall, Nichols Co. in 1910. The *Revised Ka'ai* method, which also used the "Hawaiian Guitar" subtitle, contained forty pages featuring at least a half dozen different notational conventions including chord frames, rudimentary tablature and a hierarchical chord nomenclature which has become associated with Hawaiian music; there were also detailed instructions for playing "strokes", or in the strummed style. Of the thirty plus songs and solos all but three were Hawaiian. In common with Rollinson's method were an identical graphic of an *'ukulele*, obviously related introductory material describing the instrument and its history, and a setting of Worral's *Spanish Fandango* complete with scordatura in the manner of the famous guitar piece. While much of the text is relegated to didactic explanations of the various types of notation, it is clear the author was an accomplished musician and imaginative, though pragmatic, educator who was struggling to convey his burgeoning ideas in print.

In 1914, R.W. Heffelfinger published a *Self Instructor for the Ukulele and Taro-Patch Fiddle* by George Kia Nahaolelua (1877-1929), an Hawaiian musician living and working in Los Angeles. One of at least five instruction books published for the *'ukulele* that year in California, Kia's 48 page method included chord frames and directions for strumming as well as eight non-Hawaiian songs with accompaniment for *'ukulele* in standard notation, and two *'ukulele* solos (*Hawai'i Pono'i* and *Aloha Oe*). While the publisher used the same graphic of an *'ukulele* as the earlier Rollinson and Ka'ai methods and the historical text was merely a paraphrase of the latter, the instructions for tuning were different. According to Kia, the instrument was to be tuned a full step higher than the tuning espoused by Ka'ai and Rollinson; the lower "C" tuning was to be used only for the four-course taropatch fiddle. The higher "D" tuning, which has come to be known, somewhat inaccurately, as the 'mainland' tuning, may have been introduced by Mekia Kealakai (1867-1944), a celebrated Hawaiian musician of the generation preceding Ka'ai, who led the musical delegation from Hawai'i to the Pan-American Exposition at Buffalo in 1901. Kealakai apparently authored two *'ukulele* tutors: a book of chords for *'ukulele* published in 1909, which has been catalogued by the Library of Congress (not seen) and a *Self Instructor* published in Los Angeles by Southern California Music Co. with the dual copyright dates 1912-1914. The later publication also recommended the high and low tunings for the *'ukulele* and taropatch, respectively.

The year 1915 ushered in no fewer than six new *'ukulele* books, published in both C and D tuning. One publication from *Hawai'i*, co-authored by A. A. Santos and Angeline Nunes, a granddaughter of

Manuel Nunes, advocated yet another, different tuning, that of the 'ukulele's predecessor, the machete: D g b d. While this original tuning is still used in Portugal and Brazil, it may have been revived too late and without enough proponents to catch on in Hawai'i and the U. S. In 1916 the number of new 'ukulele publications doubled, to at least twelve and the tuning duality persisted, so much so that Sherman, Clay & Co. published a collection of pieces entitled The Ukulele as a Solo Instrument in both C and D tuning written by N.B. Bailey and George Awai. Little is known of Bailey besides his publishing credits with Sherman, Clay & Co, which included a Practical Ukulele Method, a collection of songs with 'ukulele accompaniment entitled Songs from Aloha Land, and a steel guitar tutor based on the playing style of J. Kalani Peterson. George "Keoki" Elama Kaelemakule Awai (1891-1981), steel guitarist, composer and performer, was the leader of the Royal Hawaiian Quartet when they performed at the Panama-Pacific International Exposition in 1915. Awai was also the instructor at the 'ukulele display in the Hawaiian Building at the P. P. I. E. and was the director of the Royal Hawaiian Glee Club. Immediately following the P. P. I. E., Awai was an instructor in the San Francisco branch of Ernest Ka'ai's School of Hawaiian Music. In addition to his publications for 'ukulele, Keoki Awai published the Superior Collection of Steel Guitar Solos through Sherman, Clay & Co. in 1917. Containing "Full Instructions for Playing" and 48 solos in its 71 pages, The Ukulele as a Solo Instrument represented a landmark in the publishing history of the instrument. Acknowledging the 'ukulele's role "as the ideal instrument for furnishing accompaniment" Bailey and Awai felt that the little guitar had been "overlooked as a solo instrument and appreciating its

possibilities in this direction ... compiled this work." In addition to popular Hawaiian pieces and standard 19th century repertoire like Home Sweet Home the authors included college medleys, the Yale Boola of Sonny Cunha, and pieces by Gounod and Rubinstein! Perhaps the most striking aspect of this 87 year old book is its modern appearance: the music, which combines both strumming and plucking, is presented on a sophisticated dual staff in both standard notation and tablature.

Another outstanding method from 1916 was that of Ernest Ka'ai, The Ukulele and How It's Played, published in Honolulu by the Hawaiian News Co. This second method was the crowning achievement of Ka'ai's career as a pedagogue and conveyed clearly those ideas which he had struggled to elucidate in his earlier work. The method was 58 pages long, containing 27 songs with accompaniment, one duet for 'ukulele & guitar, and fifteen solos in modern tablature, eleven of which included musical notation to address what Ka'ai called the "advancement and progression" in the level of play by professionals. All but two of the pieces were Hawaiian and included several arrangements and original compositions by Henry Kailimai (1882-1948), who is remembered mostly for his hapa ha'ole tunes such as the still popular On the Beach at Waikiki. However, recent revelations about Kailimai's activities on the mainland after 1915 place him at the forefront of Hawaiian music evangelists in the first half of the twentieth century. A protégé of Ernest Ka'ai, Kailimai was selected to lead the Hawaiian musical delegation to the Panama-Pacific International Exposition in 1915. When the industrialist Henry Ford visited the Expo in the fall of 1915, he hired Kailimai's Hawaiian Quintette to come to

Detroit and perform for Ford Motor Company promotions and social events throughout the Midwest. The Hawaiian Quintette, renamed the "Ford Hawaiians," went on to record for Edison in 1916 and from 1923 to 1925 made some of the earliest mainland broadcasts of Hawaiian music on Ford's Dearborn radio station, WWI. In addition to his duties as the leader of the Ford Hawaiians, Kailimai directed the Detroit branch of Ernest Ka'ai's School of Hawaiian Music and in 1930 patented an improved guitar "steel."

No doubt referring to the works of Bailey, Awai, and Ka'ai, the Harvard Dictionary of Music remarked that "the notation for [the 'ukulele] follows the principles used in the lute tablatures of the 16th century but was invented independently." As amazing as this statement is on its own, it takes on new significance given the re-emergence of tablature in the notation of printed guitar music in the last half of the 20th century. Largely abandoned and shunned as inferior in the 19th century, the venerable system of tablature, which had served as the sole means of conveying printed guitar music since the mid 1500's, was 're-introduced' as an acceptable notational language for the guitar only some years after, and in recognition of, the sensationally popular work of the 'ukulele pioneers. Tablature, with its simple "road map" graphic style, was easy for beginners to comprehend and was well suited for conveying musical ideas on the 'ukulele, which was promoted as both an instrument "anyone can learn to play" and one which had "all there is necessary to make and cover an accompaniment for the most difficult opera written ... if one would give it complete and thorough study." Not surprisingly, the belief in the limitless potential of the 'ukulele as both a solo and accompanying instrument was not universally held, and the use of tablature was simply not acceptable to some musicians.

In 1920, the Oliver Ditson Co. introduced its second 'ukulele method, this one by the husband and wife team of string instrument luminaries Vadah Olcott Bickford and Zarh Myron Bickford. Vadah Olcott Bickford, *née* Ethel Lucretia Olcott (1885-1980), performer, teacher, author, editor and mentor, was the pre-eminent American guitarist of the early 20th century. She gave the first U.S. performances of Mauro Giuliani's *3rd Guitar Concerto*, Boccherini's quintets, and Paganini's quartets and in 1923 she was a founding member of the American Guitar Society. She contributed articles to *Cadenza, Crescendo, B. M. G.*, and other journals, and her biography appeared in the important dictionaries of Philip Bone (1914 & 1954), Fritz Buek (1926), Josef Zuth (1926), and Domingo Prat (1934). Bickford's legacy lives on through her music library which forms the core collection of the International Guitar Research Archive at California State University, Northridge. Zarh Myron Bickford (1876-1961) was a "highly educated and capable musician" (*Bone*, 1954) who excelled in performance on numerous fretted instruments, particularly the mandolin, as well as the violin and viola. Bickford was President of the American Guitar Society and American Guild of B. M. G. and a member of the Board of Directors of the Musicians' Union of Hollywood and Los Angeles. He contributed numerous articles to musical journals including *Cadenza* and *Crescendo*; his four volume mandolin method was published by Carl Fischer. Bickford's *Concerto Romantico*, written for his wife, was the first guitar concerto published in America. At 74 pages, the *Bickford Method* was the longest of the early methods and contained instructions for "all of the various styles of playing which are of practical use on the instrument, these including the ordinary Stroke Method, as commonly used by the Hawaiians, the guitar, or picking style, and the use of the plectrum or felt pick, the latter being the latest style to be developed." Flaunting their 19th century prejudices, the Bickford's made no secret of how they felt about the use of tablature, stating "any instrument which is worthy of having an instruction book written for it, is of course worthy of being written for in the legitimate musical notation, hence the diagrams so frequently given in connection with ukulele music and methods, have been eliminated from the technical part of the Method. The authors have, in their private teaching, proven to their complete satisfaction, that the diagrams are a great detriment to the musical advancement of the pupil, and that where the diagrams are readily available, the pupils invariably depend upon them, to the neglect of note-reading, with the natural result that they never become good readers. This applies not alone to those who wish to use the instrument for solo purposes, but also to those who merely take it up in a superficial manner for accompanying popular songs." However, the Bickford's were not entirely dogmatic in their approach: they notated the re-entrantly tuned fourth string of the 'ukulele an octave below pitch "to avoid confusion in reading, particularly in connection with chords employing all four strings." The difficulty inherent in notating music for a re-entrantly tuned string instrument in "legitimate musical notation" was non-existent in the tablature system, and this was probably the most important factor in the latter's widespread acceptance and use in notating 'ukulele music. While not the first to have done so, the Bickford's notational sleight of hand belied their elitist pronouncements, revealing them to be somewhat pragmatic after all, and not above bending the rules if it suited their purpose. As to the potential of the instrument, Mrs. Bickford may have found the temptation to pass judgment on the guitar's small cousin too great to resist, the guitar (and guitarists) having been mocked for generations by pianists and music critics. "No attempt has been made to make more out of the ukulele than its capacity warrants," she wrote in the Foreword. "To attempt to make it take the place or do the work of an instrument with greater power, tonal and harmonic possi-

bilities would be to call down ridicule upon an instrument which, within its limits, is effective and has given pleasure to thousands in the past and will continue to do so in the future." Such statements were no doubt in response to authors who enthusiastically compared the 'ukulele to the organ and harp "in the front rank of legitimate musical instruments worthy of serious study." In spite of their goal not to make more out of the instrument "than its capacity warrants" the Bickford's compositions and arrangements are some of the most charming and sophisticated pieces in the early repertoire of the 'ukulele.

THE MUSIC

T. H. Rollinson's setting of the traditional tune *The Blue Bells of Scotland* as a theme with one variation offered a glimpse of the solo possibilities of the 'ukulele at an early date. The arrangement includes scales, broken chords and arpeggios, and an implied polyphonic texture. More accurately described as a fragment, *The Blue Bells of Scotland* could easily have been mistaken for music written for unaccompanied violin or mandolin. The inclusion here of numerous pieces by Ernest Ka'ai is a testament to the intrinsic quality of his music and its idiomatic character with regard to the technique of the 'ukulele. Composing within the framework of a traditional European harmonic language, Ka'ai combined popular forms of the 19th century like the waltz and polka with the artistic and poetic sensibilities of a native Hawaiian. Typical subjects memorialized in Hawaiian song were people, places, events, and flowers. *Loke Lani* (the small red rose) was originally entitled *Maile Waltz* (*maile* is a leafy vine used for *lei*, particularly on important occasions) and was published in both the 1910 and 1916 Ka'ai methods. Written in a sparse type of tablature similar to Baroque alfabeto, Ka'ai expected the performer to provide the musical interest by improvising different strumming patterns which he more or less outlined in the method: "There are no set rules as to when such and such a stroke are to be used, for that is left entirely to the performer, and it is not compulsory to use one set stroke throughout a selection, a little of this and that inserted in the proper place makes an exquisitely pleasing effect." *Haele* (to and fro) is the descriptive title of a piece whose melodic line is distributed between the top and bottom strings of the 'ukulele, a style of playing known to Baroque guitarists as *campanella*. *Leilani* is a languid tango infused with *saudade*; *Hone A Ka Wai* is a lilting waltz that includes the earliest documented use of natural harmonics on the 'ukulele. While Ka'ai dedicated many of his pieces to students or friends, so that the titles may reflect some intimate meaning beyond their direct translation, he named others strictly according to their forms such as *Polka-Mazurka* and *Banjo Schottische*. George Kia's arrangement of the Hawaiian National Anthem, *Hawai'i Pono'i*, written by Royal Hawaiian Band leader Henri Berger (1844-1929) and King David Kalakaua (1836-1891), and Ka'ai's tremolo setting of Queen Lili'uokalani's immortal *Aloha O'e* are models of simple elegance. N.B. Bailey and Keoki Awai successfully presented 19th century Hawaiian standards such as *Wailana* (drowsy waters) and *Ahi Wela* (burning love) alongside popular national tunes like *Funiculi-Funicolà* and *Spanish Fandango*. Unlike Rollinson and Ka'ai, Bailey used standard tuning for his *Fandango* to great advantage, particularly in the final section where the tempo was doubled. As mentioned previously, the Bickford's foray into the world of 'ukulele music resulted in delightful arrangements like the vigorous duet *Timothy at the Husking Bee* and the original *Petite Valse* for 'ukulele and guitar, which features the instruments in a dialogue of broken chords.

THE NOTATION

All the music in this book is presented in both standard notation and tablature. Unless stated otherwise, all pieces have been notated for an 'ukulele tuned in C, however, as a practical matter, any tuning may be used. Fingerings conform to conventional classic guitar notational practices. Right hand fingers are abbreviated as follows: *i = indicio* or index finger, *m = medio* or middle finger, *a = anular* or ring finger, *r = remedio* or little finger, *p = pulgar* or thumb. Upward pointing arrows indicate strums played from the fourth to the first string (a down stroke!); downward pointing arrows indicate strums played from the first to the fourth string (an up stroke!).

THE TABLATURE

While the earliest guitarists published their music exclusively in relatively easy to understand tablature form, they struggled to find truly adequate means of conveying in print the different styles of performance possible on the guitar. The tablature system had its limitations. Quickly communicated by such simple components as horizontal lines and numbers (or letters), the realization through tablature of the *punteado*, or plucked style, with its complex rhythmic devices, particularly polyphony, was not completely successful. The notation of the *rasgueado*, or strummed style, was even less satisfactory: an 'alphabet' of letters and symbols were used to indicate chords; small vertical lines appended to the "staff" told the player when to execute strums, down or up. This *alfabeto* style tablature was generally of the most rudimentary type, often no more than simple chords played on the beat. It was left to the performer to provide the 'musical interest'. Instructions for executing the strums were usually given in the written *reglas* (rules) of the early guitar tutors, although in the actual pieces of music a skeletal framework was expected to suffice. Two strums that were often described were the *trillo* (corresponding to the modern 'common stroke') and the *repicco,* a more complicated pattern which frequently made use of the thumb.

That Ka'ai and his contemporaries had access to rare baroque guitar tablature books is doubtful. Nevertheless, the solutions they arrived at for notating the vagaries of plucked and strummed techniques are remarkably similar to those of their European predecessors. Perhaps due to a similarity in purpose, the need to ornament or embellish otherwise plain, simple tunes and harmonies with *trillo* (tremolo) and other effects, it is not a complete surprise that Ka'ai would write "Notwithstanding the fact that with the ordinary Common Stroke, the accompaniments for any piece of music could be thoroughly satisfied, yet with slight variations in the movements, the tendency to beautifying certain selections are exceedingly in harmony and most sympathetic." Also of remarkable similarity is the vagueness inherent in the early guitarist's notation of the strummed style and correspondingly, the manner in which it is treated in the first 'ukulele methods. In his 1910 *Revised Method,* Ka'ai relegates all description of the strums or "strokes" to the text, which he sometimes illuminates with diagrams. In explaining the execution of the "common ordinary stroke" (*trillo*) Ka'ai writes: "This stroke is made with the forefinger of the right hand running it rapidly across all the strings with a down and up movement of the wrist, which must be perfectly free, and keeping all the other fingers out for one position and under the palm for another position. Make the down stroke squarely on the nail of the finger and the up stroke with the fleshy part of the finger, and not on the side of the finger. There are two strokes to a beat, the down and up." Compare this to the description of the *tril-*

lo by Giovanni Battista Abbatessa (Venice, 1627): "The *trillo* is made with the finger called the index, touching all the strings downwards and upwards with rapidity."

In addition to the common stroke Ka'ai describes a handful of other strums which he then combines to produce more complex patterns. These complicated constructions have titles like "Waltz Stroke 1", "Rag Stroke" and "All-the-finger Stroke". Among the basic building-block strums are an up stroke "with thumb and [index] finger about two inches apart making a continued effect" and a down stroke "with all the fingers, beginning with the small [little] and the rest following." He also makes use of individually plucked strings interspersed between strummed chords, and partially to fully strummed chords alternated for accent and emphasis. The strums described in the following paragraphs are illustrated on page 15 in standard notation with accompanying tablature.

THE ROLL STROKE: All the beats 1, 2, 3 and 4 begin with the first finger down stroke and the half-beats up stroke with thumb and first finger (1910). This stroke is very similar to the Common Stroke, as it is not only confined to pieces of four beats, but also to those of three beats. The difference lies only in the [up] movement, when the thumb is brought to play slightly ahead of the index finger, thereby effecting a double sound with one up-sweep of the hand (1916).

THE PICK STROKE: On the first beat use the thumb, striking only the fourth string and the rest with the ordinary stroke, striking all the strings (1910). Another version of this stroke is by using the thumb again on the third beat, striking the string in the same manner as that illustrated in the first beat, thereby bringing the thumb in play on the first and third beats of the measure (1916). Ka'ai notes that the up stroke of the index finger should be "somewhat lighter, and [the down] stroke most emphatic."

THE SHUFFLE STROKE: In this stroke alternating the first and second fingers are quite permissible, the thumb however keeping its proper place (1916).

1 D With index finger followed closely by the
& D Thumb
2 U Index finger
& D Index finger
3 D Thumb
& U Index finger
4 D Index finger
& U Index finger

THE RAG-TIME STROKE: This stroke is probably the hardest of all to execute with any degree of smoothness, but with careful practice one will find it as simple as the others. Follow out closely the down and up movements, giving full emphasis on each one, only the ones with an "s" under it, then make those with a short stroke, just strike one or two strings (1910). This stroke is executed only with the index finger. The syncopated effect is produced by accentuations at irregular intervals (1916).

```
|| 1 & 2 & 3 & 4 & 1 & 2 & 3 & 4 & ||
|| D D U D D U D U D U D D U D D U ||
|| s     s         s     s         ||
```

THE TRIPLE STROKE: This stroke is done only with the first finger. There must be one stroke only on the first, third and fourth beats, but on the 2nd beat get three stokes in, without interfering with the time (1910). Use only the index finger in the execution of this movement. The triple effect coming in on the second beat, without the least interuption of time (1916).

THE WALTZ STROKE, No. 1: In playing waltz music, use one stroke for each beat, beginning lightly with an up stroke on the 1st beat and two down strokes, one on the 2nd, one on the 3rd beat (1910).

THE WALTZ STROKE, No. 2:

1 U With thumb and finger separated
2 D With all fingers strummingly
& U Index finger
3 D Index finger

JOHN KING
January 12, 2003
St. Petersburg, Florida

ACKNOWLEDGMENTS

I would like to thank those persons and organizations whose help and encouragement made this project possible: Debi King, Paul and Joan King, Pepe Romero, Paul Oldack, Sue Bober, Mark Switzer, Richard and Mary Long, Hawai'i State Archives, David Dial, Jim Tranquada, Michael Simmons, Vicki DeLeo, the Ukulele Hall of Fame Museum, Tim Mullins, Tom and Nuni Walsh, and Dolores King, who introduced me to the 'ukulele and to whom this book is dedicated.

- J. K.

ILLUSTRATIONS

Page 7: ERNEST KA'AI, *ca. 1909* (Hawai'i State Archives); Page 9: KEOKI AWAI, *ca. 1915* (collection of the author); Page 11: VADAH OLCOTT BICKFORD, *1920* (collection of the author); Page 13: GEORGE KIA NAHAOLELUA, *ca. 1914* (collection of the author).

Notation of the strumming techniques described in Ernest Ka'ai's 1910 and 1916 methods.

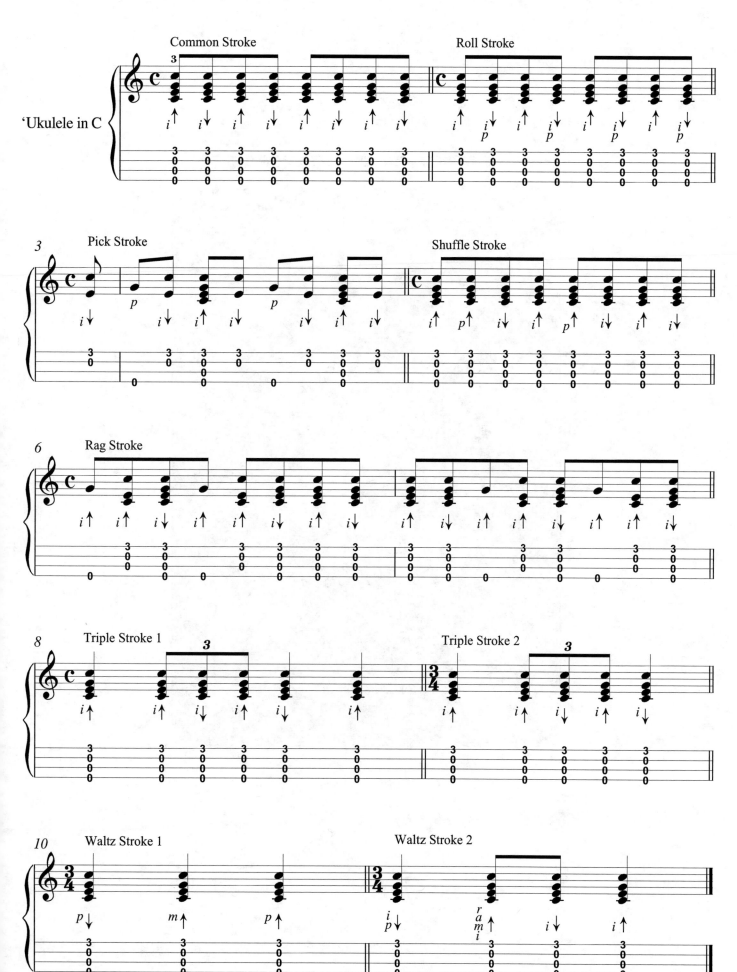

KING DAVID KALAKAUA, *ca. 1880's.*
(Hawai'i State Archives)

Loke Lani

Ernest Ka'ai
Arr. by John King

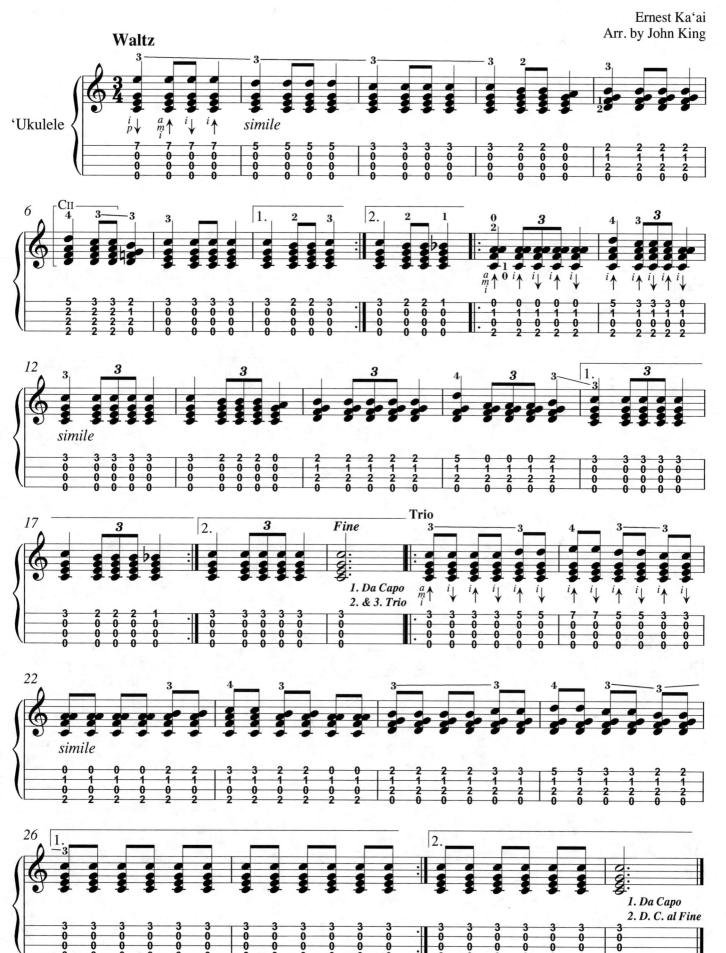

Haele

Ernest Ka'ai

Track #2

Hone A Ka Wai

Ernest Ka'ai

Polka-Mazurka

Ernest Ka'ai
Arr. by Henry Kailimai

'Ukulele

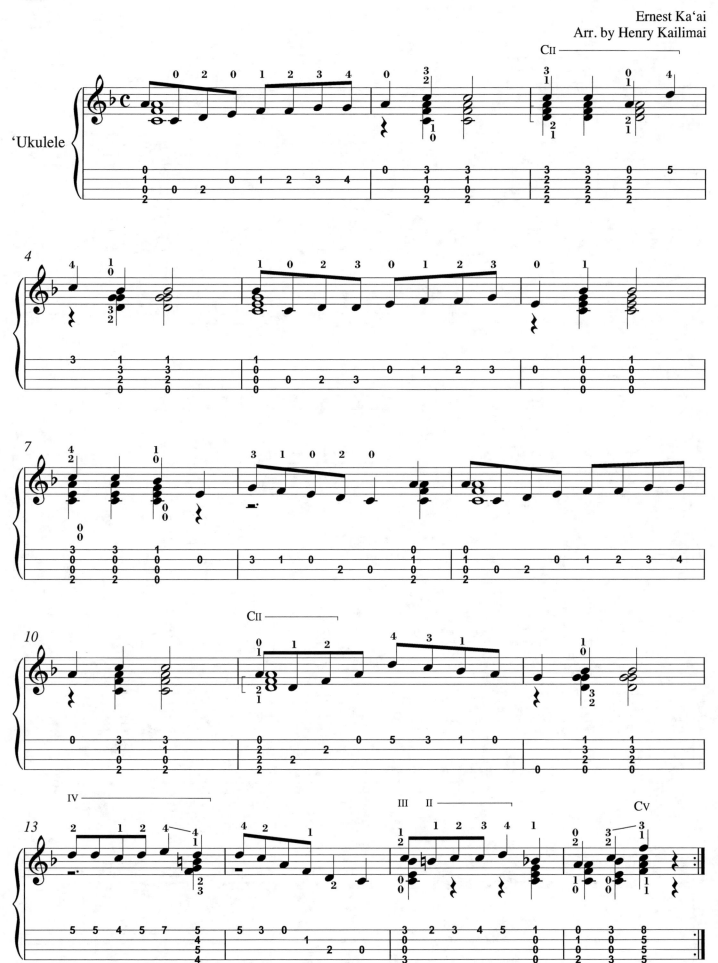

20

Ka Wehi

Ernest Ka‘ai

Tempo di Mazurka

'Ukulele

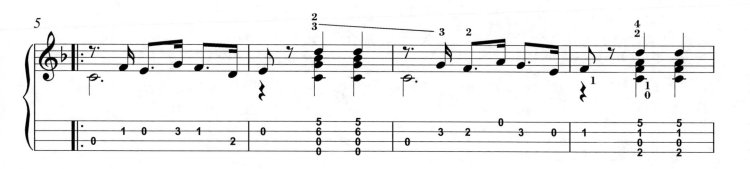

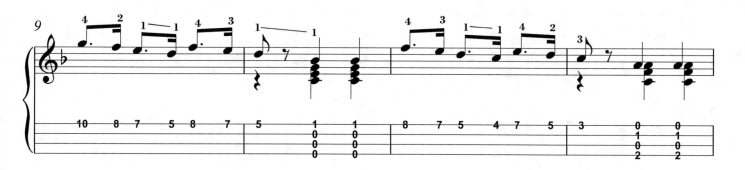

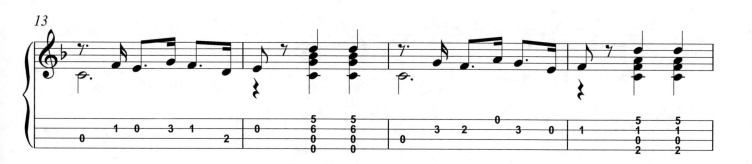

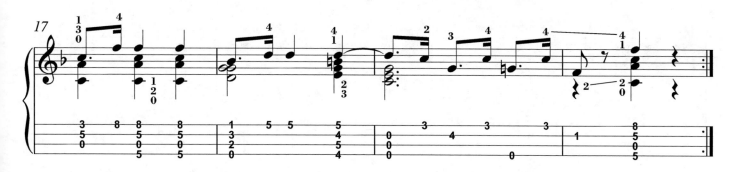

Funiculi-Funicolà

Luigi Denza
Arr. by N. B. Bailey

Track #6

22

Hene

Henry Kailimai

Waltz

'Ukulele

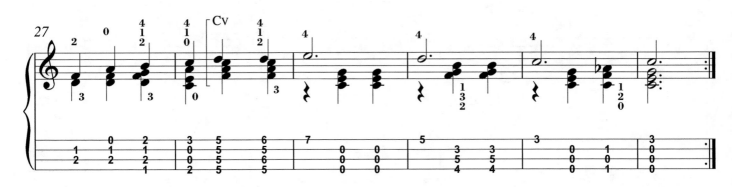

Ahi Wela

Traditional
Arr. by Keoki E. Awai

Spanish Fandango

Henry Worrall
Arr. by N. B. Bailey

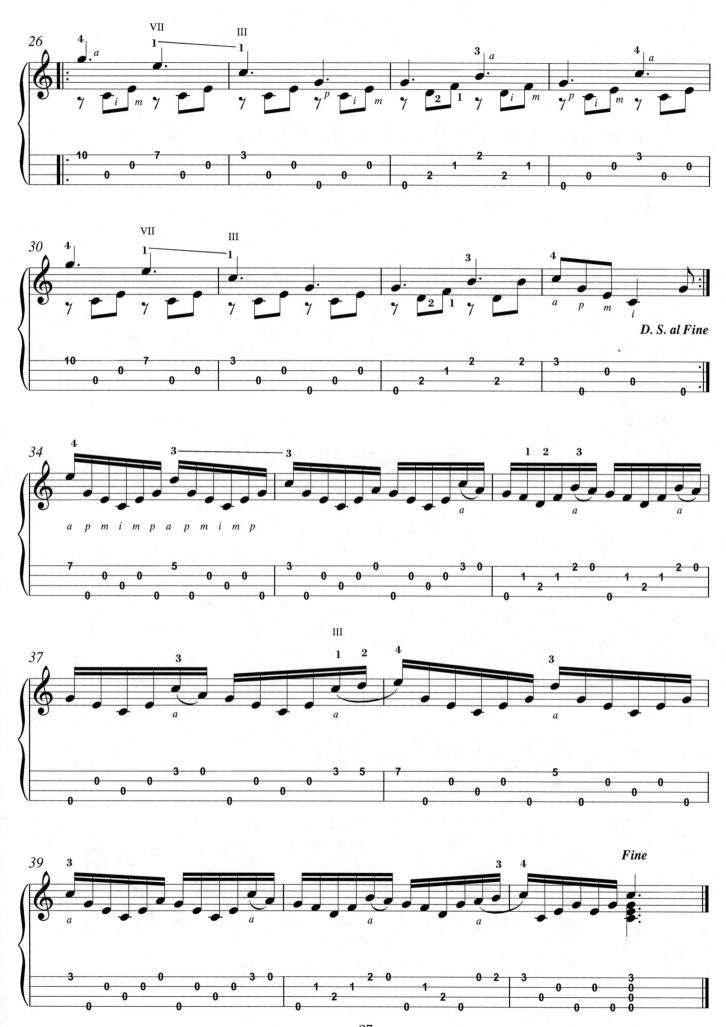

The Blue Bells of Scotland

Traditional
Arr. by T. H. Rollinson

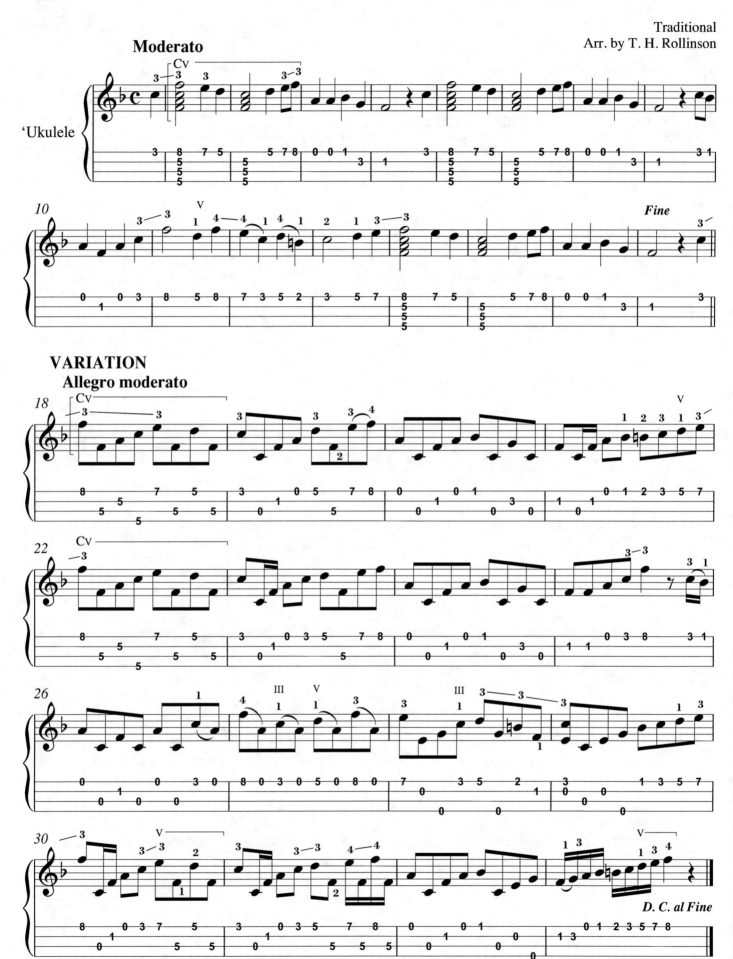

Leilani

Ernest Ka'ai

Banjo Schottische

Ernest K. Ka'ai

'Ukulele

Lauia

Henry Kailimai
Arr. Ernest Kaʻai

Wailana

Malie Kaleikoa
Arr. by Keoki E. Awai

El Recuerdo

Ernest Ka'ai

Moderato

'Ukulele

D.S. al 𝄌

Hawai'i Pono'i

David Kalakaua & Henri Berger
Arr. by George Kia Nahaolelua

Ei Nei

Ernest Ka'ai
Arr. by John King

Aloha O'e

Lydia Lili'uokalani
Arr. by Ernest Ka'ai

Serenade of the Ukuleles

V. O. & Z. M. Bickford

Allegretto

Timothy at the Husking Bee

Traditional
Arr. by V. O. & Z. M. Bickford

Fine

D.C. al Fine

Aloha Quickstep

Ernest Ka'ai

45

Petite Valse

ABOUT THE AUTHOR

John King began playing the 'ukulele in 1960 while living in Hawai'i, receiving his first instruction from his mother, an accomplished amateur. After many years of studying the technique and history of the classical guitar, he returned to his first love, the 'ukulele, with new understanding and insight. His technique has been described by critics as flawless, effortless and sublime. King's CD of Bach compositions, arranged for the unaccompanied 'ukulele and performed in the campanella style of the Baroque era, has been featured on National Public Radio and praised by the Honolulu Star-Bulletin for its "harp-like sound." Deeply interested in the history of Hawai'i and Hawaiian music, the 'ukulele, and guitar, he has devoted much of his time to research, both in Hawai'i and on the Mainland. His book *The Hawaiian 'Ukulele and Guitar Makers: 1884-1930* (NALU music, 2001) was called "the most scholarly work on 'ukulele history in Hawai'i" by the Journal of the Ukulele Hall of Fame Museum. He is a contributor to the Hawaiian Journal of History and Soundboard, and his musical compositions and arrangements for guitar have been published by Tuscany and Editions Orphée. Mr. King teaches guitar at Eckerd College in St. Petersburg, Florida.